INGLÉS PARA NIÑOS

READ ENGLISH WITH ZIGZAG -1

Copyright © 2022 Zigzag English / Lydia Winter

All rights reserved. No part of this publication may be reproduced or transmitted in any form without the written permission of the author.

ISBN: 978-1-914911-13-2

www.zigzagenglish.co.uk

OUR BOOKS FOR CHILDREN
www.zigzagenglish.co.uk

Our bilingual books for young children. *Funny stories in simple, useful everyday English, with colour photos.*
English with Tony -1- Tony moves house
English with Tony -2- Tony is happy
English with Tony -3- Tony's Christmas
English with Tony -4- Tony's holiday
My Best Friend

Our coursebook for child beginners *(age 7 to 11)*
English for Children - 1st Coursebook (Essential vocabulary and grammar for beginners)

Our series of dialogue books for beginners *(for beginners aged 7 - 11). With word lists, comprehension questions, speaking tasks and more.*
I Speak English Too! - 1
I Speak English Too! - 2

Our series of reading and comprehension books for beginners *(for beginners aged 7 - 11). With word lists, comprehension questions and more.*
Read English with Zigzag - 1
Read English with Zigzag - 2
Read English with Zigzag - 3
Read English with Zigzag 1, 2 and 3
     Audiobook - Books 1 + 2 (Audible)

The Learn English Activity Book for Children *(A1 - A2, elementary). (Recommended for children in early secondary school.)*

Our series of reading and comprehension books for children at elementary level *(recommended for ages 10 - 13). With word lists, comprehension and discussion questions and lots of language activities.*
Read English with Ben - 1
Read English with Ben - 2
Read English with Ben – 3

Our series of reading and discussion books (with writing tasks) for children at secondary school, A2 - B1
I Live in a Castle – Book 1 – The Choice
I Live in a Castle – Book 2 – The New Me

The Speak English, Read English, Write English Activity Books – *3 books from A1 to B2, for older children and adults.*

Our non-fiction book with language activities
Learn English with Fun Facts! – A2 – B2

English Dialogues for Secondary School – for ages 11 to 17, A2 – B2

OUR BOOKS FOR ADULTS

Our 3 Grammar books with grammar-focused dialogues
Learn English Grammar through Conversation – A1, A2 and B1

Our Dialogue books for adults (with vocabulary lists and comprehension questions)
50 very Easy Everyday English Dialogues (A2)
50 Easy Everyday English Dialogues (A2 - B1)
50 Intermediate Everyday English Dialogues (B1 - B2)
50 more Intermediate Everyday English Dialogues (B1 - B2)
40 Advanced Everyday English Dialogues (B2 – C1)
40 Intermediate Business English Dialogues (B1 - B2)
40 Advanced Business English Dialogues (B2 - C1)

Our activity books for adults and older children
The Speak English, Read English, Write English Activity Books – 3 books, for A1 - A2, A2 - B1 and B1 – B2.

Our non-fiction book with language activities
Learn English with Fun Facts! – A2 – B2

Contents

- Los objetivos de esta serie de libros son: 5
- Cómo utilizar esta serie de libros: 5
- Qué más? ¿Y ahora qué? 5

1 I'm Zigzag 7
2 Poppy 9
3 How many animals do you know? 11
4 Pam's a dog 12
5 Do you have a pet? 14
6 It's my sofa 16
7 Adam's hungry 17
8 I don't want to eat cat food 18
9 Poppy goes to school 20
10 Where's my toy? 22
11 School 24
12 It's not my fault 26
13 At the doctor's 27
14 I'm sorry 28
15 Birthday party 29
16 Too many boys and girls 32
17 Party games 33
18 A very small house 35
19 A weekend at the seaside 37
20 The Boss 39
21 Where are they? 40
22 I want to... 41

- Word Search 43
- Respuestas: 44
- Póngase en contacto con nosotros: 46
- Sitio web: 46
- Por favor… 46
- From: Read English with Zigzag - 2 47
- From: I Speak English Too! - 1 48
- From: The Learn English Activity Book 49

Los objetivos de esta serie de libros son:

1. Ofrecer una lectura divertida y amena.
2. Dotar a su hijo la confianza necesaria para leer en inglés.
3. Enseñar a su hijo palabras y frases clave. Los libros introducen, repiten y construyen sobre ellas poco a poco, para ampliar la comprensión del inglés de su hijo.
4. Ayudar a su hijo a aprender la gramática básica del inglés de forma sencilla.

Cómo utilizar esta serie de libros:

1. Tal vez su hijo disfrute leyendo los libros por su cuenta. ¡Estupendo! No obstante, si usted habla inglés, anímele a leer algunos capítulos en voz alta para ayudarle a mejorar su pronunciación. Hay disponible **un audiolibro de los dos primeros libros de Zigzag**.
2. Hay listas de vocabulario a lo largo de cada libro, que puede utilizar para ayudar a su hijo a aprender las palabras nuevas.
3. Encontrará preguntas de comprensión, con sus respectivas respuestas al final de cada libro. Por supuesto puede añadir más preguntas y conversar sobre la historia y los personajes.
4. Los libros incluyen actividades de aprendizaje para ayudar a su hijo con el vocabulario y la gramática.

Qué más? ¿Y ahora qué?

1. Nuestra serie de diálogos sencillos - I Speak English Too! - está pensada para aquellos padres que quieran ayudar a sus hijos a empezar a hablar inglés. Es ideal para que padres e hijos, o bien sólo los niños lean juntos. Empiece por lo más básico, introduciendo y ampliando las palabras y frases clave para ayudar a su hijo a progresar rápidamente. En pocas y divertidas lecciones, su hijo será capaz de mantener pequeñas conversaciones en inglés con usted.
2. La lectura de libros en inglés -por muy sencillos que sean- marca una gran diferencia. También recomendamos ver series de televisión sencillas para niños. Los audiolibros también son estupendos, sobre todo antes de acostarse (pues esto ayuda a retener el nuevo idioma). No espere que su hijo lo entienda todo en seguida: los audiolibros pueden escucharse una y otra vez, y su hijo entenderá más cada vez.

Early morning at Zigzag's house

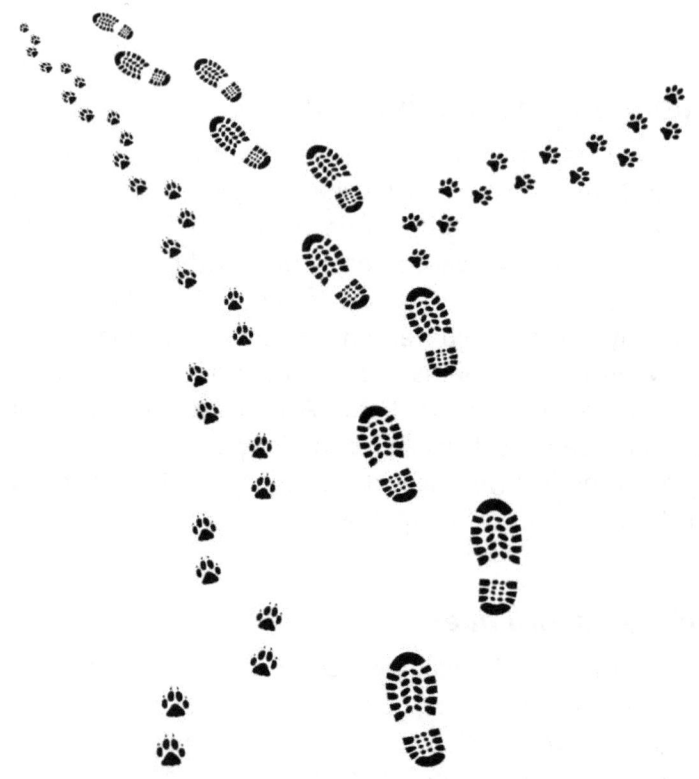

1 I'm Zigzag

Hello! My name's Zigzag. Yes, Zigzag. My name's Zigzag.

I'm six. And I'm a **tiger**. I'm not a cat. No, I'm not a big cat. I'm a tiger. I'm a small tiger.

What's your name? Are you a tiger? No? Are you a boy? Are you a girl? Are you big or small?

How old are you? Are you eight or nine? Or ten or eleven? I'm six.

I like big boys and girls. And I like small girls and boys.

I like **chicken** and **cheese**. And I like **cat food**. But I'm not a cat. No, I'm not. I'm a tiger.

I'm **busy today**. I'm very busy. I'm very, very busy. Are you busy?

I have to go now, because I'm busy. Can I see you **tomorrow**? Please? Please, please, please, please, please? Yes? Thank you!

Goodbye! See you tomorrow!

Vocabulary
- tiger — tigre
- chicken — pollo
- cheese — queso
- cat food — comida para gatos
- busy — ocupado
- today — hoy
- tomorrow — mañana

2 Poppy

Poppy is eight. She **lives** in a nice house in Cambridge. Cambridge is a small **city** in **England**.

Poppy lives with her mum and dad. She has a **little** brother. His name is Adam. He's four. She doesn't have any sisters. But she has two pets – a dog and a cat.

Her cat is called Zigzag. He's **really** big. He **looks like** a little tiger. Her dog is called Pam. She's **quite** big **too**. She's black and white.

Poppy likes playing with her cat and her dog. And she likes playing with her friends, too.

Questions:
1. Where does Poppy live?
2. How old is Adam?
3. How many pets does Poppy have?

Vocabulary
- to live — vivir
- city — ciudad
- England — Inglaterra
- little — pequeño
- really — realmente
- to look like — parecer
- quite — bastante
- too — también

3 How many animals do you know?

Where is the: hamster, butterfly, spider, rabbit, snail, fish, rat, bird and snake?

4 Pam's a dog

Hello! Hello everyone! I'm Zigzag. My name's Zigzag. What's your name? Is your name Anne? No? Is it Mark? No? What IS your name? How old are you? I'm six!

This is my friend. This is my friend Pam. Pam is a dog. I'm a tiger, **but** Pam's a dog. I'm a small tiger, and Pam is a big dog. I AM NOT A CAT!

I like Pam. I don't like dogs, but I like Pam. Pam is a good dog.

Do you like dogs? Do you like dogs and tigers? Or do you like snakes and spiders?

I'm very **hungry**. I want to **eat** cat food. Pam is hungry too. Pam wants to eat dog food. Cat food is **nice**, but dog food is **horrible. Yuck**!

Vocabulary
- but   pero
- to be hungry   tener hambre
- to eat   comer
- nice   bueno, agradable
- yuck   puaj

5 Do you have a pet?

Do you have a hamster or a rabbit? A fish or a bird? A rat or a snake?

Or do you have a cat or a dog? Which is **better**? You **choose**!

CAT or DOG?

Easy to look after?

Friendly?

Intelligent?

Fun?

Independent?

Cute?

Beautiful?

Vocabulary
- pet — mascota
- better — mejor
- to choose — elegir
- easy — fácil
- to look after — cuidar
- friendly — amistoso
- intelligent — inteligente
- fun — divertido
- independent — independiente
- cute — lindo
- beautiful — hermoso

6 It's my sofa

Hello! How are you? How are you today? Are you okay? I'm fine. Pam's fine too.

This is my house. My house is big. My house is **lovely**. Do you like my house?

This is my sofa. My sofa is very **comfortable**. I like my sofa. Pam likes my sofa too. But it's MY sofa! Go away, Pam!

This is my **kitchen**. This is my **fridge**. This is my cat food in the fridge.

I'm hungry. I want my cat food!

This is Poppy. Poppy, **give** me my cat food! Please, Poppy!

Thank you!

Vocabulary
- lovely — precioso
- comfortable — cómodo
- kitchen — cocina
- fridge — nevera
- to give — dar

7 Adam's hungry

Adam's hungry. He wants to eat:

Ice cream, crisps, biscuits, a doughnut, chocolate and sweets.

His mum wants him to eat:

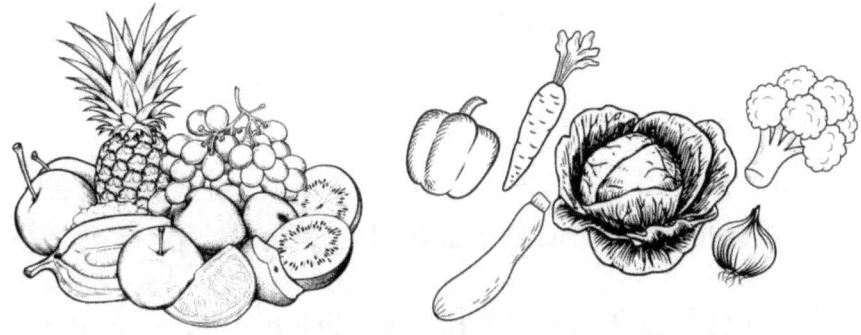

Fruit and vegetables!

Are you hungry? What do *you* want to eat?

8 I don't want to eat cat food

Hello! How are you? I'm okay today. I'm fine.

But I'm hungry. I want to eat **something**. I don't want to eat cat food. And I don't want to eat dog food. Dog food is horrible – yuck!

I want to eat... a spider! I like spiders. I like eating spiders. I like eating big, black spiders! Do you like eating spiders?

Is there a spider in the fridge? No, there's not. Is there a spider in the **garden**? Let's **look for** a spider.

Is this a spider? No, it's not a spider. It's a snail. It's a small snail. What colour is it? It's brown and white. I don't like snails.

Is this a spider? No, it's not. It's a butterfly. It's a beautiful butterfly. What colour is it? It's red, yellow and blue. I like butterflies. Butterflies are nice. They're **pretty**. But I don't like eating butterflies.

I want to eat a spider!

Vocabulary
- something   algo
- garden   jardín
- to look for   buscar
- pretty   bonito

9 Poppy goes to school

Poppy goes to school **every day**. No, not every day. Poppy goes to school on Monday, Tuesday, Wednesday, Thursday and Friday.

Adam doesn't go to school. He's too small to go to school. But he goes to **nursery**. Poppy likes going to school, but Adam doesn't like going to nursery. He wants to **stay** at home. He wants to play with the dog in the garden.

Poppy doesn't go to school on Saturday or Sunday. At the **weekend**, Poppy stays at home and plays with her little brother. Sometimes she goes to the **park**. Sometimes she goes to a friend's house.

Poppy has a **best friend**. She's called Jessica. Jessica is a beautiful name!

Questions:
1. *Does Adam go to school?*
2. *When doesn't Poppy go to school?*
3. *Where does Poppy go at the weekend?*

Vocabulary
- every day — todos los días
- nursery — guardería
- to stay — quedarse
- weekend — fin de semana
- park — parque
- best friend — mejor amigo

10 Where's my toy?

Hi! Is that you? Is that you **again**? It's nice to see you!

I feel **great**. I'm not hungry. I'm not hungry now. I don't want any cat food. I don't want **another** spider. One spider is **enough**.

Where is my **toy**? I want to play with it.

Is it **on** the **table**? No, it's not.

Is it **under** the sofa? No, it's not.

Is it **behind** the **armchair**? No, it's not.

Where is it? Oh, there it is. It's **next to** the television.

Pam, do you want to play with me? No, she doesn't want to play.

Poppy, do you want to play with me? No, she doesn't.

Adam, do you want to play? Adam? Where are you?

Yes! Yes! Adam wants to play. He wants to play with me! I love you, Adam!

Vocabulary
- again — otra vez
- great — genial
- another — otro
- enough — suficiente
- toy — juguete
- on — sobre
- table — mesa
- under — debajo de
- behind — detrás de
- armchair — sillón
- next to — al lado de

11 School

Poppy and Jessica **walk** to school with Jessica's mum.

Their school is quite big. There are three hundred and fifty children at the school. There are twenty-five children in Poppy's class and twenty-six children in Jessica's class. Jessica's class is bigger than Poppy's.

Poppy's teacher is called Mrs Rice. She's nice. Poppy likes her - most of the time!

Poppy likes **learning** English, but she doesn't like **maths**. Maths is fun, but Poppy doesn't like it. She's bad at maths, but she's very good at English. Poppy likes **break times** best. Sometimes Poppy and her friends play football. Sometimes they **chat**.

On Thursdays, Poppy takes her **swimming things** to school. All the children in her class go swimming at the big **swimming pool** near their school. Everyone loves swimming. Thursday is the **best** day of the week.

Questions:
1. Does Poppy go to school **by car**?
2. How big is Poppy's school?
3. Does Poppy like maths lessons best?

Vocabulary
- to walk — caminar
- to learn — aprender
- maths — matemáticas
- break time — tiempo de descanso
- to chat — charlar
- swimming things — cosas para nadar
- swimming pool — piscina
- best — mejor
- by car — en coche

12 It's not my fault

Oh dear. **I'm sorry**. I'm really sorry, Adam.

Does it hurt, Adam?

I'm sorry. But **it's not my fault**. It's really not my fault, is it Adam? It's your fault, isn't it Adam?

Adam is **sad**. Adam has to go to the **doctor's**.

But I want to play. Where's my toy now? Poppy? Do you want to play with me?

Please play with me Poppy! Why not? Why are you **angry**? Why are you angry with me?

I'm sad now. I'm **tired**. I'm hungry. I'm really hungry. I want my cat food!

Vocabulary
- I'm sorry — lo siento
- does it hurt? — ¿duele?
- it's not my fault — no es culpa mía
- sad — triste
- doctor — médico
- angry — enojado
- tired — cansado

13 At the doctor's

Adam has to go to the doctor's today. Poppy goes with him.

The doctor looks at Adam's **hand**. His **left** hand. There's a **scratch** on his hand.

"Is there a cat at home?" asks the doctor.

"Yes", says Adam. "I like the cat, but he doesn't like me!"

The doctor puts a **plaster** on Adam's hand. "It's not a bad scratch," he says. "But **be careful** when you play with that cat. Maybe it's really a tiger?"

Questions:
1. **Who** *goes to the doctor's with Adam?*
2. *Is there a scratch on Adam's **right** hand?*
3. *What does the doctor put on Adam's hand?*

Vocabulary
- hand — mano
- left — izquierdo
- scratch — rasguño
- plaster — yeso
- be careful — ten cuidado
- who — quién
- right — derecho

14 I'm sorry

Hello! How are you? Are you okay?

I'm fine. But Adam's not fine. **Poor** Adam.

Look at Adam's hand. He has a big plaster on his hand. Does your hand hurt, Adam?

His left hand hurts, but his right hand doesn't hurt. His right hand is okay.

Adam, can you play with me? Can you play with me with your right hand? Can you?

He doesn't want to play.

Adam, this is for you. This is a **present** for you.

It's a lovely big black spider.

Because I love you, Adam. And because I'm really sorry.

Vocabulary
- poor   pobre
- present   regalo

15 Birthday party

Poppy wants to **invite** everyone in her class to her birthday party. But her mum says no. Poppy can invite nine friends.

Poppy chooses Jessica and eight other friends. Choosing's not easy.

Poppy's birthday party is so much fun. She gets lots of presents. The best present is a toy dog that **barks.** It looks just like Pam.

The chocolate cake is **enormous**. Chocolate cake is Poppy's favourite.

Everyone sings Happy Birthday. **Some** of the children are very bad **singers**!

The party **games** are great. The best game is Musical **Chairs**. When the music **stops**, you have to **sit** on a chair. But there aren't enough chairs! Jessica **wins** that game.

Then there are **races** in the garden. Adam wins the **egg** and **spoon** race.

Questions:
1. How big is the birthday cake?
2. What do the children have to do when the music stops?

Vocabulary
- birthday party — fiesta de cumpleaños
- to invite — invitar
- to bark — ladrar
- enormous — enorme
- everyone — todos
- some — algunos
- singer — cantante
- game — juego
- chair — silla
- music — música
- to stop — parar
- to sit — sentarse
- to win — ganar
- race — carrera
- egg — huevo
- spoon — cuchera

16 Too many boys and girls

Hi there! Is it your birthday today?

It's Poppy's birthday today. Poppy is nine today.

I don't like birthday parties. They're **noisy**. They're too noisy. There are lots of children. There are too many children.

Pam likes birthday parties. She likes noisy children. She likes eating birthday cake too.

I can't sit on my sofa. There are too many children in the living room! I can't eat my cat food. There are too many children in the kitchen! I can't look for a spider in the garden. **That's right** – there are too many boys and girls there!

Mum and Dad's bedroom is **quiet**. Their bed is quite comfortable.

See you tomorrow...

Vocabulary
- noisy   ruidoso
- that's right   así es
- quiet   tranquillo

17 Party games

This is Poppy's favourite party game. It's called Musical Statues.

Play some music. Everyone **dances**.

When the music stops, everyone has to **stand still. Completely** still.

If you **move**, you're out of the game.

Play the music again.

The winner is the **last** person left.

Adam's favourite race is the egg and spoon race.

Everyone gets a spoon and an egg.

You have to put the egg in the spoon and run with it.

If you **drop** the egg, you have to **pick it up** and put it back in the spoon.

If you use **real** eggs, this race can get very **messy**!

Vocabulary
- statue — estatua
- to dance — bailar
- to stand still — no moverse
- completely — completamente
- to move — moverse

- last — último
- person — persona
- to drop — dejar caer
- to pick up — recoger
- real — de verdad
- messy — sucio, desordenado

18 A very small house

Look at this. It's a house. But it's very, very small.

I don't **understand**. Do you understand?

Who lives in this house? Very, very small **people**?

Where are the small people?

Are they **hiding**? Are they hiding in the yellow toy **box**? Are they hiding under the purple armchair? Are they hiding behind the white **bookcase**?

Is there a very small dog too? And a very small tiger?

I don't understand!

Vocabulary
- understand   entender
- people   gente
- to hide   esconderse
- box   caja
- bookcase   estantería

19 A weekend at the seaside

It's **summer** now. It's hot. It's too hot.

Poppy's **excited**. The family is going **away** for the weekend. They're going to a hotel by the **sea**.

Poppy packs her swimming things - her green **swimming costume** and her **towel**. Adam packs his red **plastic bucket**.

Pam is going to the seaside too. She's very **happy**. She takes her **ball**.

Adam puts Zigzag's cat toy in the car.

"Zigzag is a cat!" says Mum. "He can't come!"

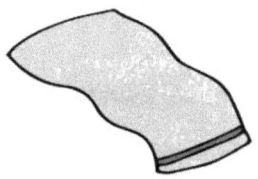

Questions:
1. Is Poppy going to the mountains?
2. What does Pam take with her?
3. Why can't Zigzag come?

Vocabulary
- sea / seaside   mar, playa
- summer   verano
- excited   emocionado
- to go away   irse de viaje
- swimming costume   traje de baño
- towel   toalla
- plastic   plástico
- bucket   cubo
- happy   feliz
- ball   pelota

20 The Boss

Hello. Is that you again? I want to tell you a secret.

Today is an important day.

Today, Mum and Dad and Poppy and Adam and Pam aren't here.

Tomorrow's an important day too. Because tomorrow, Pam and Adam and Poppy and Dad and Mum aren't here.

But I'm here. I'm in the house. Today and tomorrow, this is MY house. I AM THE **BOSS**.

And this is what I want to do…

Vocabulary
- boss   jefe

21 Where are they?

        in front of?   in?

between?   next to?

        behind?   on?

          under?

22 I want to...

I want to:

Eat all the cat food.

Chase birds in the garden.

Scratch Dad's **special** chair.

Lick the little people in the **doll's house**.

Run up and down the **stairs** ten times.

Pull the children's **pictures off** the fridge.

Bite the **next door neighbour**.

Drink water from the toilet.

Go to sleep in Mum and Dad's bed.

PURRRRRRR... That was so much fun.

Vocabulary
- to chase — perseguir
- special — especial
- to lick — lamer
- doll's house — casa de muñecas
- stairs — escaleras
- to pull off — sacar
- picture — imagen
- to bite — morder
- next door neighbour — vicino de al lado
- to drink — beber
- toilet — inodoro
- to go to sleep — dormirse

Word Search

```
Z U O I H X V F P X I L D N H
Y D H Y C E N I U E B H W E G
Z U N D E R S T A N D A W I A
G A M E N F B G Q K S E Z G R
F J F U I A T L D A L N P H D
C L P B C H O C O L A T E B E
X Q Z K G Z M F S A V E O O N
S T A I R S O R O S K C P U K
X R N L C Z R I F W U I L R O
M D Q D V O R D A M U B E Q Z
J Z K H Y Z O G E O A B X X A
G J Y C Z M W E S H P C N G Q
V F G R Y S I M L N R C D E Z
S F H M O E F Q X L Q K U O X
S U W X B A L O V E L Y H D Z
```

- It's summer. It's hot. I want to swim in the **s-a**.
- My **n-ighb-ur** has a **l-v-ly g-rd-n**.
- Why is the  in the **fr-d-e**? Because it's hot today.
- Zigzag runs up and down the **st-ir-** all day.
- I don't **und-rst-nd** how to play the **ga-e** of Musical Chairs.
- There are 2 **peo-le** on my **s-f-**! Get off, it's MY **s-f-**!
- What do you want to do **t-m-rr-w**, Zigzag? I want to eat all the cat food!

Respuestas:

2

1. She lives in Cambridge in England.
2. He's four.
3. She has two pets.

3

snail, butterfly, fish, rat, spider, snake, hamster, bird, rabbit

9

1. No, he doesn't. He goes to nursery.
2. At the weekend (on Saturday and Sunday).
3. She goes to the park or to a friend's house.

11

1. No, she doesn't. She walks to school.
2. It's quite big.
3. No, she doesn't. She likes break times best.

13

1. Poppy does. Poppy goes with him.
2. No, there's not. There's a scratch on his left hand.
3. The doctor puts a plaster on Adam's hand.

15

1. It's enormous.
2. They have to sit on a chair.

1. No, she's not. She's going to the seaside.
2. She takes her ball with her.
3. Because he's a cat.

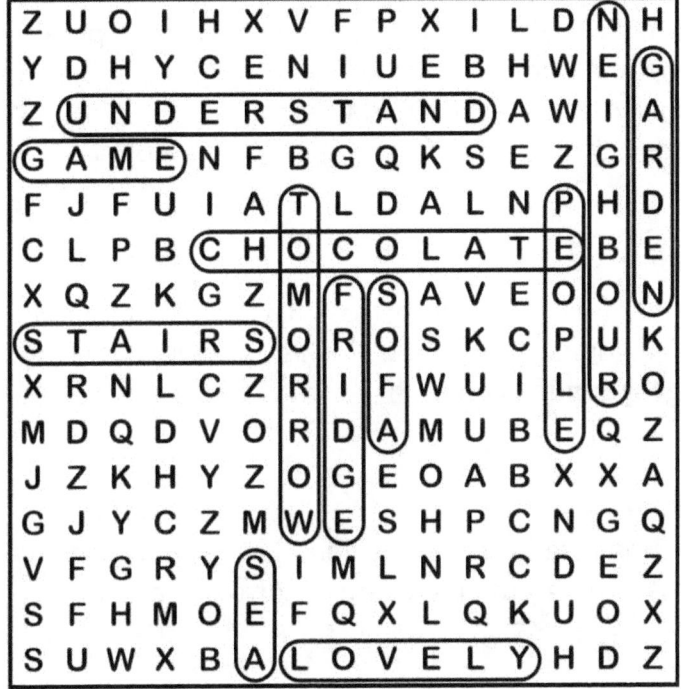

Gracias por leer este libro.

Póngase en contacto con nosotros:

Esperamos que usted y su hijo hayan encontrado este libro útil.

Si tiene alguna pregunta sobre este libro, envíenosla y nos pondremos en contacto con usted lo antes posible. Si tiene alguna sugerencia para la próxima edición de este libro, o para otros libros que le gustaría que publicáramos para ayudar a su hijo a aprender inglés, nos encantaría escucharla.

Escríbanos a: lydiawinter.zigzagenglish@gmail.com

Sitio web:

Puede echar un vistazo a nuestros otros libros para niños y adultos, jugar a algunos juegos en inglés y leer nuestro blog, en: **www.zigzagenglish.co.uk**.

Por favor...

...escribe una reseña sobre este libro. Las reseñas son importantes para otros padres y también para nosotros. Gracias.

jl

From: Read English with Zigzag - 2

5 Where is Poppy?

Hi there!

Can I **ask** you a **question**?

Where is Poppy? Why isn't she here? Where does she go every day?

Is she hiding in the house?

Is she outside, in the garden?

Do you know where she is?

I'm looking for Poppy. I'm looking for her **downstairs**, in the living-room and the kitchen. And I'm looking for her upstairs, in the bedrooms and the bathroom.

I'm looking for her **inside**, and I'm looking for her outside.

But I can't find her. Why not? Please **help** me find her!

From: I Speak English Too! - 1

6B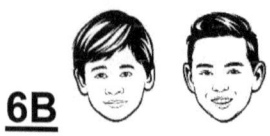

Jack: I really want a dog, Sam.

Sam: Don't you have a cat?

Jack: Yes, I do. I like my cat, but I want a dog too.

Sam: Dogs are nice, but they're very **messy**.

Jack: Cats aren't messy. But they're a bit boring.

Sam: Cats are beautiful. I want a cat, but my dad doesn't want one.

Jack: Does your mum want a cat?

Sam: Yes, she does. She likes cats a lot. But my dad really doesn't like them.

Jack: Does your brother like cats **or** dogs?

Sam: He likes **snakes**.

Jack: Snakes? I **hate** snakes!

From: The Learn English Activity Book

CHOOSE!

You can't always have everything you want.
Sometimes you have to choose.
So what do you choose?

- Ice cream or chocolate?
- A hamster or a rabbit?
- Homework or **housework**?
- A holiday at the beach or a skiing holiday?
- One very good friend or three good friends?
- Football or swimming?
- A green bedroom or a white bedroom?
- Autumn or spring?
- Chinese food or Italian food?
- Very hot **weather** or very cold weather?
- Orange juice or a milkshake?

www.ingramcontent.com/pod-product-compliance
Lightning Source LLC
LaVergne TN
LVHW051205080426
835508LV00021B/2815